Katie Sharp
Photographs by Ken O'Donoghue

A Harcourt Achieve Imprint

www.Rigby.com
1-800-531-5015

It is time to wake up.
I wake up at 7:00.

It is time to eat breakfast.
I eat breakfast at 7:30.

It is time for school.
I go to school at 8:00.

It is time for lunch.

I eat lunch at 11:30.

9

It is time to play soccer.
I play soccer at 3:00.

It is time to go home.
I go home at 5:00.

13

It is time for dinner.
I eat dinner at 6:00.